WALKING THE SUNKEN BOARDS

Walking the Sunken Boards

Poems by
Linda Blaskey
Gail Braune Comorat
Wendy Elizabeth Ingersoll
and Jane C. Miller

Pond Road Press
Washington, D.C.
North Truro, Mass.

Book design and layout: Patric Pepper

Cover photo (house with Betsy Ingersoll): Gil Ingersoll

Authors' cover photo: Linda Blaskey

Author photos (individual):
    Linda Blaskey, by Madelyn Adams;
    Gail Braune Comorat, by Joe Comorat;
    Jane C. Miller, by Paul Miller;
    Wendy Elizabeth Ingersoll, by Harvard Photography.

Additional acknowledgments follow the Notes section.

ISBN: 978-1-7336574-0-2

Library of Congress Control Number: 2019932330

Printed in the United States of America.

Pond Road Press
Mary Ann Larkin and Patric Pepper
221 Channing Street NE
Washington, DC 20002
pepperlarkin@juno.com

Available through Amazon.com and other online
booksellers, and through Pond Road Press.

We dedicate this collection to our husbands,
in grateful appreciation for their support on the home front
while we pursue muses.

And to Gil and Betsy Ingersoll, whose spirits welcome us.

Contents

Poems by Jane C. Miller

Poems by Wendy Elizabeth Ingersoll

Preface

The cover photo of *Walking the Sunken Boards* is of Betsy
Ingersoll, Wendy's mother, in 1944, posed in front of
the small farmhouse she and Wendy's dad, Gil, built
at Shipping Creek Farm, their property on the Chester
River on the Eastern Shore of Maryland. Over the
years since, the house has been expanded and revised
to take full advantage of its 360 degree view of river,
cove, fields, meadows, orchard, and creek.

For the last few years we four poetry-writing friends have
met there biannually for a long weekend: writing, reading,
revising, giving feedback, doing poetry-exercises, taking long
walks, lying in the hammock, gossiping, eating, and laughing.
We call the house and our weekend there The Muse. And
when we are not in residence, we are looking forward to
our next gathering.

Walking the Sunken Boards is a compilation of poems written by
the four of us, all of which were begun, revised, and/or fin-
ished at The Muse. The house is what holds us to
look out and look in.

Linda Blaskey

LINDA BLASKEY'S work has appeared in numerous journals and anthologies including *Best New Poets 2014.* Her work was also chosen for the North Carolina Poetry on the Bus project and has been nominated for a Pushcart Prize, Best of the Net, and Bettering American Poetry. Her chapbook, *Farm,* was published by Bay Oak Publishers, and was a winner in the Delaware Press Association's Communications Contest. She was a finalist for the Patricia Dobler Poetry Award, and a winner in Third Wednesday's One Sentence Poem contest. She is the recipient of two fellowship grants from Delaware Division of Arts and is poetry/interview editor for *The Broadkill Review* and coordinator for the Dogfish Head Poetry Prize. She grew up on the plains of Kansas and in the Ozark Mountains of Arkansas. She now lives in the flat lands of southern Delaware.

As the Dock Goes Under I Think of You

The river is higher than it has ever been and I desire
to put on boots, walk the sunken boards;
a daring or a testing of what is deemed real.

An egret lands on the few inches of piling still above surface
but doesn't tarry long, wary—
like when we hover our hands over a lit burner,
feel the heat, pull away.

I am on land observing the rising level of the river,
can place my hand on the oak and feel anchored.

But what of seafarers in open water, their source of bearing?
It is hard enough to maneuver love's hidden bulkheads—
how do you trust this tide.

Shipping Creek Farm, 3:12 A.M.

Lying on her side in the bed
she looks out into the night.

She sees her own countenance
reflected in the window pane

but knows the water
is out there, large.

She tries to dream
that she is paddling a canoe

to that little hook of land
just over there. It beckons

like an embrace, and she is sure
that's where butterflies land

on sunflowers, open and close
their wings with a certain melancholy.

There are some things
that she just knows—like

how you can't force a dream;
that broken plates can be mended

but are never the same; that he
will soon leave. She can feel it

in how he turns his back to her
in sleep, the way he eats breakfast

behind newspapers. She already misses
the tiny scar, new-moon shaped,
that rests on the blade of his shoulder.

Another Mode of Self-Defense

The sun has dragged its shimmer across the river,

shore to shore I've watched it go;
have lain here, bland in head, followed its progression—

hawks cry, wind scuffles, still I stare
until retinas sear a blur in center vision.

Go ahead and try to lay me low;
I've made your face a plate scrubbed clean of all expression.

Another look upon the river, beauty in the burning.

Tall Ships

I have been promised them, their splendor,
canvas bulging in effort to push them upriver.

So far only small trawlers, a tug alone,
not unusual sights for an eastern tide.

The water is silver from sun filtered through cloud-cover
and the morning chill feels hard as dimes.

There is glint like false promise in the air,

like another kind of waiting—waiting
for the right man to come along. So many
before you think you have it right

only to find all you want is sleep, not this
new waiting for his bearish back to stop heaving,
for his pungent sweat to evaporate,
for the suck of his pulling away.

On the river the wind has picked up.
The awaited ships now must travel under motor-power,
sails furled, spars like bones.
Already, I plan for disappointment.

Detritus

You've left your dishes on the counter for me to clean up again.
I haven't put the lid on the peanut butter jar in the right way.

Your socks are everywhere and I wish you'd shave on the weekends.
I've left the car low on gas, and isn't it my turn to feed the damn cats?

We've been bickering for days and I want to flee
to higher ground, like I fled the carcass of the dead dog washed ashore

by last night's spring tide. The body was skeletal, the limbs
and metatarsals contracted but the head was intact, still covered in hide,

lips pulled back in a snarl as if fighting to the end.

What to Do with an Old Loveseat

I've been standing in front of it
for so long the room has gone dark.
It belonged to a friend long dead.

It had a settled life with her but a hard one with us.
Certainly never cuddled on by you and me, and under
our thin replacement slipcover it is rent by cat's claws.

From the corner of my eye, something white
moves beyond the window and for a moment
I think it is snowing.

But it is seventy degrees in September
and the movement is two white horses,
tiny like toys, in the back pasture.

A red-shouldered hawk sits on a fence post waiting
for prey. Yellow jackets circle the compost heap
in search of something sweet.

How I Came to Finally Understand "Lying in a Hammock at William Duffy's Farm in Pine Island, Minnesota"

Consider the cove, how an arm of sand
reaches around, calms the river's turbulence.
This is where osprey have chosen to nest.

I push with my foot and the sun winks
from behind the birch's canopy.
Leaves applaud the breeze.

In full sun, a woman sits at the dock's edge,
her hair a shimmer of silver.
She has made herself small—
knees tucked to chest, arms around knees,

perhaps drifting in thought
as she watches her face change
in undulations of river water.

Inside the house someone whistles an aria
from *Carmen,* the famous one everybody knows,
the one with descending notes.

A Walk to Gil's Grave on His Ninety-Fifth Birthday

Grasshoppers scatter before my feet,
bouquets of sulphurs and painted ladies
hover over the buffer zone
of cone flowers, susans, wild yarrow.

A swallowtail lands
on a yellow flower I can't identify,
dips its proboscis deep into the bloom.
I lean in and watch it beat its ecstatic wings.

Gil's ashes are interred
around the next bend
in a grotto of trees between
Danger Cliff and the rise where Conkey's house
was to be built, but never was.

From his resting place, I turn
in a circle, see everything—

He grew up on a farm a mile upriver
and his boyhood friend, Jim Faulkner,
lived over there, near Quaker Neck Landing.
A whiff of diesel fuel from fishing boats
drifts across the Chester

to where Gil's daughter, in a hat
her mother wore, gazes across the chop,
the wind moving her skirt like the grasses
that sway along the shore.

I Wait for Him to Return
from an Old Friend's Funeral

—she was looking sideways....to the right
—where they say the unlived life is.
                    Marie Howe

Steam of goats' breath streams upward as they browse wintering
blackberry vines.

Debris from last night's storm litters the yard.

For this evening's hearth, I gather downed twigs
        and manageable branches
into an empty bucket, the arc of its handle pressing my right hand.

I worry about him driving in this weather,
about taking the truck when the car has better traction.

Everything is still and I wonder if this is what it will be like, after.

I turn my head, look to the frosted lane for approaching exhaust;

only fragile ribs of fish float in the cold sky.

Poem Written by the Side of the Road

I have stopped to fill my eyes with this field
for you—rapeseed blossoms, acres golden

as the yolks of the eggs you served me
this morning on a plate edged with sky.

Cabbage-white butterflies drink the nectar,
their proboscides deep in the flowers'

dark centers, while above goldfinches,
mated for life, sing their *sweet sweet*
and feast on the oily seeds.

Yellow is the color of hunger. Feed me.

Sometimes There Is a Sadness

The door ajar, a slim finger of light
reaches over worn ashwood floor—

I hear his toothbrush
drop into the holder,

the swish and spit into the sink;

hear ticking of plastic cup
against tooth enamel.

How his hand now trembles
as he takes his last drink before bed.

Chopin Ballade in G Minor

When I am old I want to sit in this wicker chair
with this book open on my lap, these slippers on my feet,

and gaze through this glass wall at the lagoon
placed like a silver coin on the landscape,

and listen to this music which sounds perfect
to my ear though the pianist claims to have made
many mistakes.

Gail Braune Comorat

GAIL BRAUNE COMORAT is a founding member of Rehoboth
Beach Writers' Guild (RBWG), and the author of *Phases of
the Moon* (Finishing Line Press). A Pushcart nominee, she has
twice received Delaware Division of the Arts fellowship grants
for poetry. Her work has appeared in *Gargoyle, Grist, Mudfish,
Philadelphia Stories, The Widows' Handbook,* and numerous
anthologies. In 2012 she won the Artsmith Literary Award for
her poem "Summer of Ladybugs." She's a long-time member
of several writing groups in Lewes, where she teaches poetry
and grief-writing classes for RBWG.

Where You'll Find Me

I'm no good at route numbers, never sure of east
or south, but I know this road by seasons, by landmarks
memorized the last time I traveled this way.
If you still want me, just head away from the city,

keep an eye out for meadows of bold blue and yellow—
bachelor buttons, wild mustard. Cross the rusted iron bridge
that will lead you to a crossroad—
turn left and keep going until
you see a stand selling Tender Spring Peas and
an orchard of peach trees beyond their bloom. Take your time

as you roll through the old mill town
where elderly men in suspenders and felt hats
doze on planked benches. Wave as you drive by.
You'll pass beneath a thick canopy of elms, and then

there will be a Mennonite farm (one with yellow siding
and pine-green shutters)
with a misspelled sign that offers *Saw Sharpning*.
You might see a few deer in the field.

After that, it's straight on until the road dead-ends
to a graveled lane. Drive as far as it takes you,
park right beside the house.
I'll be on the crooked swing,
rocketing skyward and back, skyward and back,
my eyes on the cove, watching
bald eagles query the river.
I'll be waiting for you.

The Fox at Shipping Creek Farm

His image at the window
doesn't startle us. He reflects
a certain calm, a curiosity.
Perhaps the amber light

of the house intrigued him.
Perhaps he's come to listen
to our poems. He sits politely
on the other side of our world,

a wild prince with a steady gaze.
And beyond here, the river
continues its work in darkness,
just as this fox must soon move on

to do the work all foxes conduct:
the hunt for small creatures moving
silently, trusting in their safety.
We shuffle papers in a room

surrounded by land, sky, and water.
Sycamore and cedar. A rising
gibbous moon, an owl calling.
This is our brief haven

inhabited by deer, osprey, and
this glorious fox who now stirs
from his haunches, and shambles
toward the woods.

There's just enough light
for us to notice his hobbled gait;
he is missing his left hind foot.
Still, he proceeds with purpose,

moves with all the majesty
his imperfection allows. And
inside this farmhouse, we slow
our own pace, stumble over
our praise with dumbstruck awe.

The Body Is Not

a colored illustration in a science text,
not a flattened pocket containing all
that we are, an androgynous outline
with celluloid sheets we lift
to reveal the muscles, the veins,
the glossy white bones. And

neither is my friend's body a city
despite the way her scans light up
like a runway with night descending.
Like looking down on BWI,
she says when she shows me
her body's dark transactions:
a map of bright mushrooms
displayed in brutal radiance.

—*for Allyn*

In the CVS Beside the Hospital

I'm searching the beauty aisle for a miracle
to fix crow's feet, reading a package that says
Corrects and Reduces All Signs of Aging when
I realize I've teared up, and I wonder if it's because
of the headline on a nearby journal proclaiming
THE DEATH OF BUMBLEBEES with its close-up
of a bee in mid-air. I wipe my eyes, search the label
seeking retinol and amino peptides, key words
to make me believe and I know I'm a fool to worry
about my appearance when my friend is losing
her hair in clumps, buying wigs she can't afford
and already mourning the loss of lashes and brows.
This same friend who urged my bids on a Wyeth
remarque at a museum auction, who convinced me
to buy my first summer house, my darling friend
who made me take a test drive in a convertible
that was too impractical. Each time she said,
Do it. Don't we all deserve beauty in our lives?
Suddenly I hate the bees and those doomsayer
forecasts, and I don't see how what might happen
to them affects me, but my eyes are burning and
I can barely see, so I make my way to the exit,
where I trigger an alarm and the woman behind
the counter glares at me until I realize I'm still
holding a box of Regenerist Eye Lifting Serum,
and she's asking, *Are you gonna pay for that, hon?*
I root through my purse, grab bills, push them at her,
not caring the cost. I'm sobbing, the salt of my tears
drying my mouth, and I'm certain the cashier thinks
I'm crying from guilt, that I'm crying from shame
and I want so much to tell her that I'm just crying
for the goddamn bees.

The Diameter of a Ringling
Bros. Circus Ring

after Yehuda Amichai

The diameter of a circus ring is forty-two feet,
an arena large enough to contain three elephants,
three performance stands, two trainers, and
a ringmaster. And inside this ring, each elephant,
upon her designated turn, turns circles around
the ringmaster as he cracks commands with his
ceremonial whip. And no more than ninety feet away,
eight other traveling elephants wait in a steel-
barred cage of insufficient measure. And in this cage,
they hear the cries of their sisters as they perform
a shuffle around the ring, their soft-soled feet scuffing
dirt into the circus air. The caged elephants shift and
shoulder each other, bellow back, setting off a call
and answer of all elephants, a shared chain that
becomes wild notes rising and falling outside and
inside the big top, where the master's sharp whistle
sends children scuttling closer to their mothers, and
the mothers circle their little ones with rounded arms
as all the elephants repeat their circle of song. And
the song rings and rings and lingers even after
the canvas walls come down.

Invisible Man

Some days she sees him in
her periphery

                              his one-word sign
                              propped against
                              an empty grocery box

she drives by on the way to the salon
late for her hot stone massage
        When she was a child
        she learned to avert her eyes
        from roadkill

Sometimes as she absentmindedly
ticks off her to-do list
        can-can sale at Giant
        oil change at Jiffy Lube
        birdseed and pansies at Ace
she notices   he's not there

                              no plea scratched across
                              a scrap of discarded cardboard
perhaps he's relocated   moved on
to another post

Today   he's back
outside Starbucks

                            hungry

she sees him
in the rearview mirror
as she lowers Ray Bans
to shield her eyes
from the glare

he holds the word
aloft

she turns off
the satellite news
when talk turns
to burning fields of poppies
in distant Kandahar

The Forgetful Woman Attempts a Pastoral

On the way to a Wawa
I pass bucolic views of horses,
hay rolled into wrapped coils,
farms with names: Fairywood,
Uphill Farm, Briar Parry.

I need a toothbrush.

No other store is near, so I'm driving down
a country road where trees form a canopy.
It's late autumn, and the branches are mostly bare.
The rush of my car scatters tinted yellow leaves as I pass.
Once, we painted our bedroom the same shade of gold.

Didn't I tell you on our first date
that with my passport and toothbrush
I was ready to travel anywhere? Yet
here I am, far from home without
a simple necessity. These days
I'm too easily distracted.

Not a cow in sight. The horses in the fields are dark
and graceful. Not sturdy animals built for farming.
Their coats gleam. A few wear quilted blankets
across their backs.

I woke to gun shots this morning.
Not unexpected for a rural area.
And after all, it's deer season.
Deer are everywhere. I drive
slowly, not because the road
is unfamiliar or because it snakes
through the woods, but because
deer often stop in mid-crossing.

When we met you were a hunter, taxidermied ducks
on tables, shotguns on your walls. Now you hobby
at vacation-planning. Weren't you just last month
plotting our trip to Barcelona?

My tires crunch small twigs and black walnuts
still in their hulls. I remember how my father
collected the fallen bounty every autumn, how
his strong fingers worked to break them open.
The cost of black walnuts was steep, but oh
how he loved the taste of them in pound cake.
How can he be gone almost twenty years?

I'm at a dead end. This is where my friends said I'm to turn right,
and when I do, countryside becomes a small town with a traffic circle
and the Wawa. Inside, I stand in line with utility workers in polyester
jumpsuits. The man behind me is Jimmy if I go by the stitching
on his pocket. He's buying a hero sandwich, shaped like a torpedo
wrapped in white paper.

That same week you were finalizing hotels
in Spain, the attack in Las Ramblas made you
scrap your plan. You said, *When did vans
become weapons?* Last week, a massacre
in a Texas church. *The world is too full
of danger,* you said as you helped me
load the car with books and groceries
for this trip on my own.

I ride past grazing fields once more, as I head back
to my friend's river house, to other poets writing in their rooms.
I look forward to afternoon chatter in the kitchen, to eating
bad food and staying up late talking about the necessity of poetry,
art, and music in this world we're sharing.

Last night the moon was a hazy
scythe dangling in my window.

The Last Man on the Moon

The dock is submerged again. Rain
and tides have swelled the cove.

If you were here, you'd tell me again
about gravitational pull,
about neap tides.

What was it you loved?
Waxing crescents? Once upon a
blue moon
you loved me. If you were here,

I'd like to think
we'd wait together

for waters to ebb,
for the dock to come back.
We'd hold hands,

dangle our feet the way
we did last fall. I'd ask you again
the name the Algonquins

gave to this rising full moon—
even though I remember

it's called the Dying Moon.
If you were here, you'd tell me

the story of the astronaut
who etched into the moon's dust
his daughter's initials.

I wonder if they're still there.
Just as I'll always wonder

if you've erased my name
once inked in radiant blue
crescent-curved upon your shoulder.

A Little Night Romance

She said, That moon is too magnificent for the sky.
Yes, a man could drown in its light, he replied.
But after all, he was a sailor who'd once lived
upon rolling waves. She understood his need

to recall, to romanticize his sailing days.
There are so many names for the moon, she said.
The moon transforms itself; it transforms us,
he said. But, really, he was thinking about

the Ama, their naked moon-round breasts
as they emerged from their deep dives
for abalone and oysters. They rose from water,
glistening and shivering. Primitive.

Tail-less Japanese mermaids, harvesters
of seaweed and turban shells. He'd seen them,
plumbing the Pacific. Young girls in loin cloths,
filling their lungs with air, disappearing

from the dock of a small village. His mouth
had been a soundless moon. All around him,
fellow sailors wore the same slack jaws.
A lifetime ago, but still he remembers them.

To her, he says, We are not meant
to live in water. No one could breathe
in such beauty. And she's certain
he's speaking of true love.

The Sea Wives Speak of Love

Red-lit skies, the lullaby swish of sea. Crashing stars, their loops and prongs swaggering in the night. Brash and god-like in their fall. One by one, their icy whiteness summons us topside. Our hearts beat and blaze like brides in their season.

A life on land offers only saplings to plant. Rather we spend weeks on wild seas. We become glass to keep horizons steady. Secrets fall amid the ropes. Beds become unsteady, we time our breaths between the swells. We'll take it all. Isn't it enough to live the pitch of years, to be in love with the rough planks of this restless ship?

November at the Muse

We've packed long underwear and
heating pads to warm our sleeping bags.

Outside, the wind drives down
withered brush rimming the cove.

For three days we write in solitude,
eat when hungry, share prompts

for inspiration. Wrapped in wool
against the cold, I sip pumpkin-spice tea

in my garret and search my Mac's
thesaurus for the perfect synonym

for heaven. The view from my window:
a bright sky from the gods. An arrow-straight

line of ducks zips by, the sun catches
the white chest of a gull as it wheels above

a solitary dock standing in wind-beaten water.
This morning we witnessed a whitetail

leave a spit of land to ford the river.
Tonight we'll need a fire to heat the den

when we gather to listen to each other's work.
In spite of our complaints of chilled hands

and lines that won't come, we write,
make poems from small moments. Like now

as a computer chimes in a distant room, I scrawl
words on my tablet like someone called to prayer.

Prayer

At my daughter's city home
I watch a soundless flight of cormorants
skim a rubbed-chalk sky
toward Smith's Creek, their number uneven.

A year of ups, downs. Yet I know this life that dazzles
and disappoints is our rosary.
We must touch and worry each moment in the knotted
strand that separates us.

I unclip wash from her backyard line
as a cool rain begins to fall. Above, the birds string out
like loose black pearls
tossed randomly across these ever-shifting heavens.

Jane C. Miller

JANE C. MILLER'S poetry has appeared in the *Iron Horse Literary Review, Summerset Review, cahoodaloodaling, Watershed Review, Mojave River Review, Pittsburgh Poetry Review,* and *The Broadkill Review* among others. She has been nominated for Best New Poets, Best of the Net and was a finalist in the 2017 Red Wheelbarrow Poetry Contest as well as the 2018 Florence C. Coltman Award for Creative Writing. She has received a fellowship and an honorable mention in poetry from the Delaware Division of the Arts and is a member of several writing groups including the Written Remains Writers' Guild in Wilmington, Delaware.

Fall Morning/Shipping Creek Farm

I set my coffee to boil. Behind the stove,
frost makes a mountain on the windowpane.

Spice jars rise before it like a city block
of red-capped buildings, all owned by McCormick
except the black pepper mill with its button-top
like a bishop's biretta, a worship center.

Outside, a Canada goose trumpets
the world heavy with red sunrise.

Coffee in hand, I watch.

A doe swims the cove,
her head and backbone moving
above wind-puckered water.

It reminds me of us in bed,
only our heads visible. Dreaming,
we too travel our hard routes.

Each clock in the cabin tells
a different time. Snowshoes face-off
above a door frame. Two ducks stuffed in flight
wing the walls. Painted boats tack their sails full.

Outside it is hunting season
and into this landscape, we write ourselves.

Evolution Is a Funny Thing

The field-mouse, a grey dash
across the door sill
thins himself
to disappear behind the stove.
Somehow he knows tomorrow
will be the coldest yet,
23° F with wind chill.

I smear peanut butter on the trap,
leave it parked on a paper towel
(a place setting for one)
and go to waiting sleep—

one ear to the ground, (a skill I learned
when still a wife) listening for that man
to gravel up, to chug his bulk upstairs
to anchor his side of the bed.

Nothing disturbs but my bladder.
I creep downstairs. No peanut butter. No mouse.
The trap not tripped, but pushed around.

Three nights later, he lets me watch.
His dexterity all tail, he dips it into the bait
and turning it with the skill of a circus master's whip,
offers his mouth a taste.

I know he is vermin but I am still a sucker
for the wrong kind.

At table, his yellow teeth devour
Gouda, Laughing Cow.
He never uses his tail anymore,
not even as a napkin.

I feel my nose thin, my face turn feral.
In the wall mirror, his eyes dart
to my date-nut muffin. What did I see in him?

Behind the sugar jar, I still have poison,
what's left of it.

No Beginning One Middle Two Ends

We passed a stick in the grass, a black-barked stick
but then saw halfway down
the jaw of a snake

wide and snug
one of his kind half-devoured in his mouth,
the eaten almost as big around as the swamp-dark

swallowing one, whose size we guessed at eight
unyielding feet,
his black eyes angry bulging wet
his tapered tail shaking the marsh reeds.

We had disturbed his lunch—
our exclamations and photos kept a safe distance—
and wondered as it was natural to do

what kind of snake was this, that could cannibal
what hatched from an egg like him, that grew strong on rabbits,
squirrels, fish.
What drive would drive him but instinct?

Mid-feast, he shrugged himself back
to tall grass, dragging his crime scene with him
the ambush, the victim

tug of skin on skin
the way men do women they have had
enough of

Café

Let's say you are young too,
and she is only a couple years older,

maybe working as a server
where people never stay long,

but she doesn't come forward
to take your order or even bus tables.

She stays in the back by the register,
crying and pacing and seeming to wait

for her crying to stop on its own,
which makes her look what we used to call

slow, but her crying doesn't stop
because grief takes a body as its own

and this is her occupation now.
You want to say, "What's wrong?

It will be okay," but her cries are a language
you don't yet know. And you think,

"She probably just lost her job,"
something she can replace.

So you leave to shop for a purse, to catch
a train, and only when your father dies

and then your mother, do you see
you have carried her all these years

and when you look in the mirror,
you see her face. This time,

you offer tissues.
You do not look away.

Afterward

The dock is almost under again, its uprights
like faces upturned before vanishing.

Since you died, days press their throttling tide
and each night, darkness pours its panic marbles
underfoot and I walk the house, let myself out

to prowl the sleeping cove and come back
to stand at the refrigerator, searching
in the alien light of its kitchen moon
for solace, but there is only water.

From the icebox, small coffins chill my glass
and a carafe, lipped like my body, dies
of thirst as it drains. I drink and drink,
but there is never enough swallowing
that can save me from air.

On the Yangtze

Nets stand like fences
    awash in the river

Ancestor fish
    —finned palominos—
nose mollusks, rope-bound

Currents sway
    in the sun's pink wash

On my fingers, nicotine—
    on my shirt, ash
        where it slept

I watch one water
    become another

How Our Bodies Carry On

Every cell is an old woman bent
with bones bundled on her back,
their scars indelible
as scrimshaw, fretwork hidden
in yellowed cracks left
by the undoing: femur
from hip ball, humerus
from shoulder claw. Every
uplifted limb breathes napalm
as memory, carbon monoxide
as scream. Bodies blown
and tossed like rice.
Every cell, a delta
an old woman picks through.

Caesarian

I held her captive, suspended in a diving bell
                as if to shelter from calamity this child
        inside me like an organ I couldn't live without,
            for every birth begins a eulogy.

    But they cut her loose from the bubble
                where I had talked to her,
            where she tapped
                    morse code for months.

Post-delivery, they sewed her absence into a finish line.

    Every year after: a racing bib
                with candles for numbers.
        I let her go as I should,

but let no one tell you it is easy.
    The wound where once I cradled her
        a buckled scar.

To My Son Gone to War

My call to dinner is lost in the din
of bombs and downed men.

Did dropping Super Mario down pipes lead us
to this *Call to Arms* where you die

and die again, when it's life
I want to keep you in?

What labor foretold, the push
of head against bone,

and following a suctioned plume, breath—
how your birth cry bloomed to curdle time.

I was your first
casualty, your newborn hands

tight-fisted as fiddlehead ferns,
hung heavy as bell clappers

as you grew. I cannot blame you

for playing soldier to kill or maim,
for I know the thrill

of waiting for what's hidden—
the boredom, the blast, the pain.

I am on the losing side,
but still yell *I have mac & cheese,*

your favorite. I will forgive you
everything if you come to me.

Stranger

after Jo McDougall

When happiness came to visit,
I invited him in. He drank

the best wine, all the beer
in the garage refrigerator.

I would have thought
he would not need such an escape.

But turns out, he has a hard job.
He has to steer conversations clear

of all grief. He has to be jolly.
He thought I would be happy

to feed him steak and pommes frites
in the French manner—a salade verte

and Costco cream puffs for good measure.

They are good, but I had
to set limits. Ours is a double bed

and I am a married woman with a dog.

Ode to Fado/Lisbon

Her back against the restaurant wall; men cradle guitars
that cry lonely as footfalls on cobbled streets. From her voice,
the smoky lamentation of hardship and church pews centuries
of sweat have darkened.

She sings of narrow alleys; a brazier, its coal fire smoldering
sardines salt-sharp and crisp-fried, enough to fill a small plate,
though hunger is large as ten mouths in one room. Hunger
at the door screaming for rent; for what's lost, a candle to St.
Anthony, a shot of ginjinha.

She sings of laundry lines, towels that snap between buildings
like ship flags; with saudade, she salves the hands hard-cracked
from bluing to rid cotton ribs their bruise of stains.

In her song, notes cast themselves down stairs headlong.
There, a child coughs and coughs, his temperature soars his
body to shake and sweat through his underwear, and no one
sleeps for the scare he will climb out of bed into death.

In Mouraria, she hums the heart's tattoo of walls that locked
the Moorish people into night, fado their song to mourn loss,
their mosque toppled for Lisbon's oldest church.

She sings the River Tagus that dragged thousands and half the
city in a tsunami to its depths. As her voice sweeps over us,
hear their cries and weathered tears fall on Convento do Carmo
that survives without its roof.

With longing, she shakes the prison bars of Salazar's victims,
chimes the bells of cathedrals and wooden trams.

Everywhere fugitive roses striving for sun, she praises them.

Letter to Her Husband in the Next Room

If all the world were you and me,
would we ever be enough? You engulf
the latitude and longitude of me
as a tree does its sun-making
shadow. Soft the carpet that warms
my feet upon rising. My robe you bought
is a silk scene: peacock feathers
fan my back, and in front, I cinch a mist
of sky larks, as if fore to aft,
I wrap us together. Coffee you made
dark as a well fills me. Mouth
to cup, I think of night, your lips soft
and soundless traveling down
to ravish my voice's urgent unraveling.
What gluttony, this whorl of touch.

The red oak lightning-blasted
still blossoms a gnarled shadow.
May we last that long.

Wendy Elizabeth Ingersoll

WENDY ELIZABETH INGERSOLL is a retired piano teacher whose publications include her book *Grace Only Follows,* which won the National Federation of Press Women Contest; two chapbooks; and poems in various journals, for which she's twice received Pushcart Prize nominations. Other contests include first places in the John Milton Memorial Celebration of Poets and Poetry, the Delaware Literary Connection, and Rehoboth Beach Writers' Guild, as well as finalist in the Dogfish Head Poetry Prize. She also enjoys serving as reader for *The Delmarva Review.* She grew up in Hockessin, Delaware, and lives there now, periodically visiting Shipping Creek Farm.

Among the Irises

Every Easter weekend at our farm by the river
the bunny hid jellybeans.
My sister and I found them on dusty window sills,
behind the salt and pepper shakers, between

napkins in the wooden basket
on the long trestle table that was my grandmother's.
We'd pop them quickly in our mouths—
sweet was rare in our family. After the hunt

I always went to church with my cousin Rachel.
I'd dress up in violet velveteen dress, white gloves,
white straw hat with the little veil.
My dad would take our picture,

waving among the irises running riot by the tractor shed.
Going to church made Easter
more than just a chocolate binge followed by
inevitable egg salad. I felt like normal people

from a normal family that didn't scream or throw dishes.
The church had stained-glass windows parading the Gospels.
During the sermon I studied the glass people—so tasteful,
halos in place, with hair

that didn't frizz.
I fell in love with church.
I don't understand now
what god I was worshiping,

surely not the one who attended my wedding,
Father Perkin's god who took my groom aside
and warned him not to wed a Protestant.
Nor was my childhood god the one who

shrugged his shoulders when my sister
lost a second child, as if to say
What do you expect me to do about it?
And not the god who assigned my dad to lose

all memory, pockets of his brain turned
holey, everything sifting through. So many
gods there are out there,
like the wild geese who filled the sky

flying home those Easter weekends when I was young.
Who can tell which god to pray to,
or if our one true god will just know
how to find us where we hide?

In-Season

I know the difference between people and deer, he grunts,
as he strings his bow and slams shut
the hatchback. Dusk:

the pines by the pond lane
line up like lineage, each reaches
to block brothers, sisters from sun, or offer shade. I shift

to scan the next row, scout its distinct
vista, assess limbs and cones, check underfoot
for salamanders, copperheads—destiny,

when we can recognize its breastbone, its spine,
is a walk between trees.
I sight a fawn,

tiptoeing wide-eyed, ears erect
as I blend with bark. What is the difference?
Like a shot—biker:

skinny pants and helmet,
vying to pass or mow me down—should I
be pedaling? My fawn disappears. All of our span

we wander rows of pine,
questing for a better view—
there are so many days

when up and down the chain it's open season,
all we can do is wear orange.

Loon

We floated across the hour our mother died
like the heron in our cove
skims water.

We lay on the bed beside her,
    waited to see if she'd return.

At last we rose, opened
closet doors, pulled out
one dress after another,
selected one for death
she'd never worn in life.

She would have chosen the fuchsia,
immersed herself in hue,
as the loon dives deep in our cove.
    Before she left

we asked her to fly us again that glance,
the lone way all our lives she spoke of love.

But she only lay there quiet,
    swimming beneath the surface.

Fisherwoman

Except what we've forgotten, we remember everything—
sand bar in light rain, tide slides in, finger on the line
as I cast, lure paraglides above, alights,
bobber begins slow rhythm with the waves, and then
your search alone along the current, sudden lunge
at lure, bobber ducks and weaves, quick
jerk of my hands, line sears, reel spins,
cranks, we're in each other's sight,
tie between us taut til you're exhausted, I reach for net, scoop,
and you're here.
                      You rest
on sand, breathe
as well as possible, like all of us in our peculiar school—
we females live as proof
that everyone leaves, husband, children
swim away at turn of tide, leave us spent and netted,
splayed gasping on the cutting board,
gutted heads and hearts, barbs through lip of rib,
what could we know
of plunging, drenching love, what can we do
but try to thread the day
like line through bobber, sinker, lure?
                      Now all that's left
is to pull the hook from your lip
with least harm, my best intention
to send you back to the stream, no hard feelings—
let's both continue with our day, me floundering above,
you idling beneath the surface like all the
cruelty and conceit I've ever cast into the sea.

Tomato Boat

a painting by Emma Hess Ingersoll, the author's grandmother

Skipjack, my cousin claims.
Long beam, single mast far forward, trunk cabin just aft.
But it's the tomatoes that claim my eye:
bushels and baskets, lined up on deck and dock,
ripe rubies. Two men in overalls bend and lift.
Above, sails are furled, rigging slashes the sky.
Beyond, the river curves from Quaker Neck to Shippen Creek.

Here on this landing stood my grandmother,
erected her easel, licked her brush to a point.
Artist and mother, she painted my father
in miniature on ivory,
in watercolors sailing the river,
in oils a young man in a blue tie.
She painted him until she died.

My father's old, his only memory is of his mother's touch.
As if a wave rose on this river, the ship pitched,
and tomato on tomato spilled overboard,
skins split, seeds washed away. River red.
I have a host of bushel baskets stacked on deck—
impatience, ingratitude, intemperance—
all ripe, ready for shipping. God take

every one of them—the times I shouted at my father,
the aid I begrudged him, the hugs I never gave, the days I
wished he'd die. When I was a girl
I thought tomatoes would forever taste as fine
as the ones he grew on our farm.
I'd run down the rows, pick a fat one warm
from the sun, twist it off its scratchy vine,
eat it juice dripping from my chin.

Clutch

When the tractor stalled on the hill
as I was giving my granddaughter
steering lessons,

we all rolled backward: she, me,
all my family in the wagon behind,
down the hill, speed increasing,

family shrieking, my right foot
thrusting at both
brake pedals, left foot unable to reach clutch

even as brakes failed
completely, tractor and wagon
hurtled backwards, tipped,

curved 'round like a cupped hand,
jackknifed, we all stopped
dead.
        It reminded me

        of just before I never drank again—
systems failing, me accelerating in reverse until

the tipping point, a cupping hand, and I came to rest,
scared but still.

My Father's House

Before he died
my father's memory floated away like flotsam on tide.
My last visit we sat on lawn chairs back of the house
that Dad called the front,

breathed brine of river's swell,
studied herons spearing pike among the cattails,
tasted not quite the catch stacked in the crabber's dingy
looping trotlines offshore—

and Dad turned to me and begged,
Take me home, I want to go home.
I said here is home, and he cried out,
No, the home where Mother is—

my family. Now four of us, all but one,
gather to bury his ashes
back of the house, the front,
and ponder our missing one

who'd blurted hurt against our rite,
emptied from the bag of ash
one fifth's amount,
swore to scatter it

a good stone's throw away.

When the Postman Refuses to Deliver Mail

to my cousin's box across the road
and under a myrtle straddled by roses,
cause so many ants brawl inside
that whenever he stuffs the phone bill in
he fears assault,

my cousin calls the Post Office.
She asks about her options.
Cut down the tree they say,
our computer will not allow
variation of mailbox location,
it's programmed in.
My cousin's face
gets red as she tells me.
Changing a mailbox,

like changing a tire,
a diaper, a husband,
is not so easy we agree.
I begin to get a bit red in the face myself.
My group reminds me weekly
it's not in my job description to mend the planet,
nor even the Eastern Seaboard. But
nothing comes cheap, not even

mail. That night
driving past my father's broken-down box
I turn the headlights off, follow blackout
up the lane. I think I see his shadow,
familiar, trudging ahead.
I speed up, night quickly
fills in the spaces, he's gone. Sometimes

we need to look sideways
to see in the dark.
Agnes Smith, who owns the field
beside our lane and across from my cousin,
swears she'll cut that myrtle down, raze the roses.
When I lose Dad I pull over,

scan her land: rows of corn stalks
chopped off at the knees, drowning
in yellow weeds. The opposing side
is orchard, grass waving high,
sea without shore, pear trees struggling
above the surface, trunks submerged.
Maybe that's where Dad

hides. In the end my cousin confides
in the postal powers. Her phone bill now is delivered
to a new box at her gate, no ants,
contented mailman. I'm seventy years
and I know what I know, which is sometimes
it's *Who* you know.

Between Me and the Far Trees

a drainage ditch draws a straight line
down the middle of the field and into
the next, collecting sticks, bugs, clots of earth,
spilling them onward the way Bach
floats a phrase into the next measure,
the way forgiveness
must be ferried into tomorrow.
So I paddle forward that moment

my husband said he was leaving. At dark
this ditch is where my father would scout,
snap on his torch to shine in the eyes
of a big bullfrog hunkered in the mud,
retinas reflecting the light until
he shot between them with his 22. He mostly stalked
ducks—in the house there hangs from the ceiling

a clean-shot mallard, wound
patched, wings spread, dead head
glossy-green as new spring leaves.
It was traveling a line south or north,
wanting, like us, warmth or propagation,
when it spied our field, circled.
Now it floats below our ceiling,
looking as if it longs to land.

I Cross the Neuse

to reach Days Inn after the game Friday night:
the floods below have slowed their tumble and topple,
there's barely a skim of foam, as if
deepest waters lift stillness to the surface.
Everything I have ever known

my seventy years of life I'm doggy-paddling through,
like uttering again the name
of someone unaddressed for twenty years:
strange and yet familiar as my image
backwards in the sideview mirror. Before he died

my father whispered his life to me
and I made daughter-poems, not always
sweet. Crossing the Neuse, I conjure
me riding shotgun on the tractor, feet
braced against the axle shield and Dad
alive at the wheel—we pass the last row

of stalks and husks, cross the county line, chug west
across the Bay Bridge, high above heave, we never
queue at the booth, never pay the toll,
we just keep rolling like the wide Bay beneath,
watch it make its own face anew with every
groundswell surging up from deepest brine
to sun and air.

Weekend at the Farm

What's that? I ask my father.
Mockingbird, he says. *He sings a song three times
then changes to a different tune—
that's how he mocks us, by the changing.*

It's rained all day like Noah.
Dusk has checked it—the sky's still scabbed around the edge
but blank in its center as a closed door.
My shadow, long as lies in the telling,
follows me down to the river's gentle hand.
Tide's brimmed high—dock planks float in the cove.
A wood duck thrusts from the rushes,
veers hard left, black head pointing through the late-day air.
In the corner of my eye a minnow leaps.
I turn my head but nothing's there except
a circle blossoming on the glass—
perhaps the center of the circle
is the center of the world—
the minnow's silver leap sets all in motion,
river, farm flowing from the round.

I was a mirror in my former life.
I lived like a simile.

This afternoon in the cottage
I nested the old china in the cupboard that leans,
tall as my father once,
in the cool, white corner of the room.
I twisted the latch, loose from years of turning in its place,
scanned cracked plates, patinaed trays.
When my father was ten,
he was tossed over a fence by a bull.
Never turn your back on a bull, he's told me,
showing me the blurred scar scaling his shin.

Evening is setting its table with shadows.
Yesterday we see only as through bone china. Tomorrow
waits in the night cupboard.

Distance is what my eye wants now.
Even the sun, with distance, fades to just another star.

Listening with the Left Hand

Sunset on the estuary is orange.
Our side dish for dinner is everything
dug-up—naked carrots, blind potatoes,

onions unwrapping like Magi gifts.
I'm thinking of tattooing a plus sign on my shoulder,
like a little chip.

We swim through space,
carrot peeler in hand,
earth falling, river rising. If we resolve,

dessert can be berries and cream.

Notes

"Lying in a Hammock at William Duffy's Farm in Pine Island, Minnesota" is a poem by James Wright.

"Among the Irises," "Between Me and the Far Trees," and "Tomato Boat" appeared in Wendy Ingersoll's collection *Grace Only Follows* (March Street Press, 2009).

"Deciding What to Do with an Old Loveseat," "How I Came to Finally Understand Lying in a Hammock at William Duffy's Farm in Pine Island, Minnesota," and "A Walk to Gil's Grave on His Ninety-Fifth Birthday" appeared in Linda Blaskey's collection *White Horses* (Mojave River Press).

"The Diameter of a Ringling Bros. Circus Ring" won Honorable Mention in Philadelphia Stories' Sandy Crimmins National Prize in Poetry, Spring 2017.

"Between Me and the Far Trees" won the 2008 Delaware Literary Connection's Susan Clapp Jamison Award.

In "Ode to Fado/Lisbon" the phrase "fugitive roses" is from "Odes" by Fernando Pessoa (Ricardo Reis).

Acknowledgments

Grateful acknowledgment is given to the editors and staff of the following publications in which some of the poems first appeared, a few in slightly different versions.

Bay to Ocean: The Year's Best Writing from the Eastern Shore: "Caesarian," "Stranger"
The Broadkill Review: "Shipping Creek Farm, 3:12 A.M." "When the Postman Refuses to Deliver Mail"(as "Getting Mail"), "I Cross the Neuse"(as "Crossing the Neuse")
cahoodaloodaling: "In-Season"
Delaware Poetry Review: "Among the Irises"
Delmarva Review: "Tomato Boat"
GAMBA: "No Beginning One Middle Two Ends"
Mojave River Review: "Loon," "Another Mode of Self-Defense," "Tall Ships"(as "Waiting for the Tall Ships"), "Detritus," "In the CVS Beside the Hospital"
Naugatuck River Review: "Fisherwoman"
Peacock Journal: "The Fox at Shipping Creek Farm," "Listening with the Left Hand"
Philadelphia Stories: "The Diameter of a Ringling Bros. Circus Ring"
Poetry East: "Clutch"
Rat's Ass Review: "Afterward"
Red Eft Review: "The Body Is Not," "Prayer"
Red Wheelbarrow: "To My Son Gone to War"
Summerset Review: "My Father's House," "As the Dock Goes Under I Think of You," "Sometimes There Is a Sadness"
The Sow's Ear: "Café"
Third Wednesday: "Chopin Ballade in G Minor"
Writer's Journal: "Weekend at the Farm"
Your Daily Poem: "Where You'll Find Me"

Thanks to Clayton Adams for his work on enhancing the cover photograph for printing.

Special thanks to Patric Pepper and Mary Ann Larkin for believing in *Walking the Sunken Boards,* and for their dedication in bringing the book to fruition.

Colophon

The title font used for this book is Amarone. Amarone has been described by MyFonts.com as a "spiky calligraphic display typeface," combining a contemporary elegance and formal character with the charm of old-fashioned pen and ink. It was designed for Monotype by Carl Crossgrove, and released in December of 2018.

The body text is set in ITC Galliard, created by the renowned British type designer Matthew Carter. It was originally issued in 1978 by the Mergenthaler Linotype Company, and has since been redesigned and expanded for international and eBook use. Based on the sixteenth-century type of punch cutter Robert Granjon, Galliard is noted for its sheer beauty, legibility, and distinctive italics. It is routinely used for both display and body text applications.

This book was printed by Ingram Book Company (Lightning Source Inc.) in the United States of America.

Also from Pond Road Press

Messages, by Piotr Gwiazda
Parts & Labor, by Gregory Hischak
Radio in the Basement, by Bernard Jankowski
Familiar at First, Then Strange, by Meredith Holmes
Shubad's Crown, by Meredith Holmes
Blue Morning Light, by David Salner
Human Animal, by Anne Becker
Crooked Speech, by Sid Gold
Tough Heaven: Poems of Pittsburgh, by Jack Gilbert

Available online from Amazon.com and other online
booksellers, and from Pond Road Press directly.

Email us at
pepperlarkin@juno.com
patric.pepper@yahoo.com
pondroadpress@hotmail.com

Printed in the USA
CPSIA information can be obtained
at www.ICGtesting.com
LVHW092349300823
756635LV00044B/97